LIGHTNING
BOLT
BOOKS™

Big Rigs
on the Move

Candice Ransom

Lerner Publications Company
Minneapolis

To Bill, who's gonna make it home tonight

Lerner Publications Company
A division of Lerner Publishing Group, Inc.
241 First Avenue North
Minneapolis, MN 55401 U.S.A.

Website address: www.lernerbooks.com

Library of Congress Cataloging-in-Publication Data

Ransom, Candice F., 1952–
    Big rigs on the move / by Candice Ransom.
        p.   cm. — (Lightning bolt books™ — Vroom-vroom.)
    Includes index.
    ISBN 978–0–7613–3919–9 (lib. bdg. : alk. paper)
    1. Tractor trailer combinations—Juvenile literature. I. Title.
    TL230.15.R365 2011
    629.224—dc22   2009039738

Manufactured in the United States of America
1 — BP — 7/15/10

Contents

Big Jobs

It's a new day. This big rig is already on the road.

Big rigs have many names.
You might call them
semitrailers, tractor-trailers,
or eighteen-wheelers.

Can you guess what
these trucks are hauling?
Big rigs carry cargo.

These big rigs carry
cargo in their trailers.

Big rigs can carry horses. Big rigs can move barns. No job is too small or too big for a big rig.

A big rig can move an entire house!

Big rigs can carry just about anything. Auto carriers haul cars. Tanker trucks carry liquids, such as milk or gas.

An auto carrier brings new cars to car dealerships.

Flatbed trucks haul extra big loads. Big rigs can tow up to 60,000 pounds (27,215 kilograms).

Big rigs even carry new rigs!

One big rig tows three more behind it.

The back of this big rig is refrigerated. It keeps cargo cold and fresh.

This refrigeration unit keeps the trailer of this refrigerated truck cool.

Big Parts

Big rigs have two parts.
The driver sits in the tractor.

A driver stands in front of his big rig's tractor.

The tractor pulls the trailer.
Cargo is put in the trailer.

The trailer hooks to a metal plate on the tractor. The metal plate is called a fifth wheel.

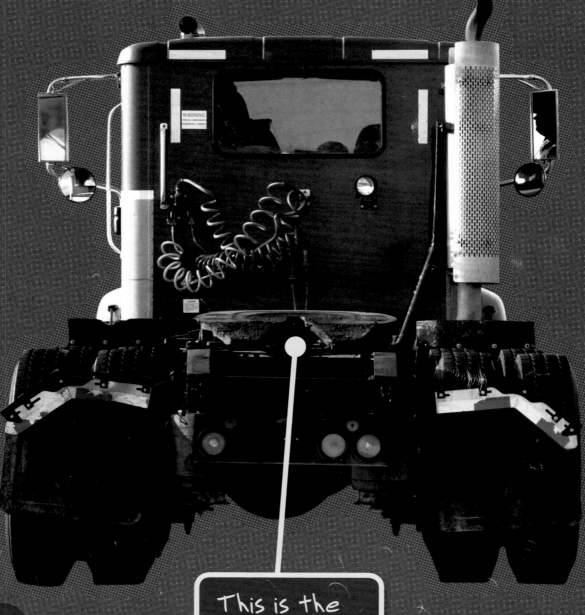

This is the fifth wheel.

Trailers stand on legs called landing gear. The driver hooks the trailer to the tractor and cranks up the gear before driving away.

Built to Go

Big rigs go wherever there are roads. Big rigs rumble through forests.

A logging truck hauls tree trunks.

Big rigs cross bridges and climb mountains.

17

Snow and ice won't stop this truck. Big rigs are built to go.

On steep hills, trucks may go too fast. To stop, drivers can steer onto sandy roads. These ramps slow down trucks.

This ramp is on a mountain in Colorado.

Rig Truckers

Truckers can call for help on a radio called a **CB**. They also call one another to talk. They have their own language. "Ten-four" means yes. "Hammer" is the gas pedal.

A trucker talks on his CB radio.

Big rigs run on diesel fuel.
They use a lot. Drivers get
more diesel at truck stops.

Truck stops are more than gas stations. They have restaurants and even showers!

Some truck stops have books that truckers can borrow.

Everything about a big rig is big! The steering wheel is bigger than an extra large pizza.

Most big rigs have eighteen
wheels, nine on each side.

This rig has
twenty-two wheels!

The trailer's wheels
come in sets of
two on each side.

Big rigs are so
big the driver has to
stand on the tire to
reach the engine.

The inside of the tractor is called the cab. It is so big that a bed can fit inside. Truckers pull over and sleep in the cab on long-distance trips.

This cab has a bed and a television.

Day or night,
Big rigs are on the road

Big Rig Diagram

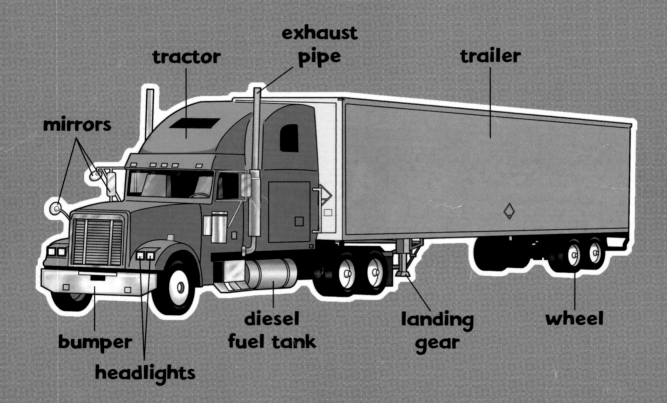

mirrors

tractor

exhaust pipe

trailer

bumper

headlights

diesel fuel tank

landing gear

wheel

Fun Facts

- A tractor without a trailer is called a bobtail. It weighs about 19,000 pounds (8,620 kg).

- A tractor can tow 60,000 pounds (27,215 kg). It would take five hundred or six hundred horses to pull that much.

- Most big rigs have two tanks for diesel. Each holds nearly 150 gallons (570 liters). That's as much as three hundred jugs of milk. It's so much that drivers need to refill only once from New York to Los Angeles.

- In trucker language, a police officer is called a bear.

- The engine in a big rig is four times bigger than the engine in a sports car. Big rigs travel slower than regular cars, because big rigs are too heavy to go faster.

Glossary

cab: the driver's place in a truck

cargo: the boxes or things carried by a truck

CB: a radio that can send and get messages. Drivers use CBs to talk to one another.

diesel fuel: a type of thick gasoline

engine: the machine that gives a big rig power

fifth wheel: the part of a big rig that connects the front to the back

tractor: a truck that has an engine and a cab

trailer: the part of the big rig that carries things and is towed by the truck

Further Reading

Brecke, Nicole, and Patricia M. Stockland. *Cars, Trucks, and Motorcycles You Can Draw.* Minneapolis: Millbrook Press, 2010.

Lyon, George Ella. *Trucks Roll!* New York: Atheneum Books for Young Readers, 2007.

Make a Truck
http://www.enchantedlearning.com/Slidetrucks/Slidetruck.html

Manolis, Kay. *Big Rigs.* Minneapolis: Bellwether Media, 2008.

Morganelli, Adrianna. *Trucks: Pickups to Big Rigs.* New York: Crabtree, 2007.

Index

Photo Acknowledgments

The images in this book are used with the permission of: © James Steidl/Dreamstime .com, p. 1; © Richard Leeney/Dorling Kindersley/Getty Images, p. 2; © Robert Pernell/ Dreamstime.com, p. 4; © Walter Hodges/Digital Vision/Getty Images, p. 5; © Tom Paiva/ Taxi/Getty Images, p. 6; © Edmond Van Hoorick/SuperStock, p. 7; © fotog/Getty Images, p. 8; © Robert Harding Picture Library/SuperStock, p. 9; © Gary Blakeley/Dreamstime .com, p. 10; © Dary423/Dreamstime.com, p. 11; © Seth Joel/Taxi/Getty Images, p. 12; © age fotostock/SuperStock, p. 13; © Nancy Tripp/Dreamstime.com, p. 14; © Robert Cabrera/Dreamstime.com, p. 15; © Bob Pool/Photographer's Choice/Getty Images, p. 16; © Frank Whitney/Photographer's Choice/Getty Images, p. 17; © Andrea Pistolesi/Riser/ Getty Images, p. 18; © Henryk Sadura/Dreamstime.com, p. 19; © Jupiterimages/ Workbook Stock/Getty Images, p. 20; AP Photo/Phil Coale, p. 21; AP Photo/Enid News & Eagle, Billy Hefton, p. 22; © Marc Romanelli/Workbook Stock/Getty Images, p. 23; © Eugene G. Schulz, p. 24; © Robert Carner/Dreamstime.com, p. 25; © Todd Strand/ Independent Picture Service, p. 26; © Jeremy Woodhouse/Digital Vision/Getty Images, p. 27; © Bill Hauser/Independent Picture Service, p. 28; © David Mcshane/Dreamstime .com, p. 29; © Mauritius/SuperStock, p. 30; © Robwilson39/Dreamstime.com, p. 31.

Front cover: © Timothy Passmore/Dreamstime.com (top); © Robert Pernell/Dreamstime .com (bottom).